Godly Character

Bible Study
for Women

Denise Gilmore

ADISAN Publishing AB

Table of Contents

Introduction

Reading the entire Bible in a year is not an easy task. There will be many distractions that will keep you from reading every week. There will be weeks when you don't feel like reading God's word, or you will simply forget to read it. There will be weeks when you will be so glad that you took the time out of your day to read His word. As you take on this new study Bible, I want to encourage you to take it one step at a time, one verse at a time, and one week at a time. If you ever miss a week, don't punish yourself. When you feel pressured to catch up on a few weeks, remind yourself that it is not a marathon. You don't have to put pressure on yourself to catch up, nor do you get points if you finish before the full year is done. Just keep going and pick up right where you left off. Ask God to help you commit to reading this study Bible as often as you can and simply let God do the rest of the work in your life.

The design of this plan is to let you read a new scripture every day, so you can learn more about who God is and what His character is really like. You will read portions of epistles, law, history, psalms, poetry, prophecy, and the gospels each week. Before you get started on this journey, it is vital for you to know what each category means. The epistles are letters written to various people and churches after the life, death, and resurrection of Jesus. The book of laws are the first five books of the Old Testament that tell us what to do and what not to do according to God's word. In those readings, you will learn about the different laws that the Lord instructed people to obey, and you will also learn about the origins of God's people. The history portion tells us all about the past of God's people, who they were, and where they came from. The book of Psalms is one of the most influential books of the Bible, and you can spend the entire year just reading the Psalms Day by day if you want to. The Psalms are where people cry out to God in praise, prayer, anger, and even love.

The poetry section will tell you about the concerns, pains, and wisdom of God's people. The prophecy section is where people foretold about God's love and Jesus' birth, life, death, and resurrection thousands of years before He was even born. Forth telling is where people proudly proclaim what the Lord is doing in their lives and in the lives of others. Lastly, you will read a portion of the Gospels each week. There, you will find many eyewitness accounts that talk about the life, death, and resurrection of Jesus. You will also read through many of the eyewitness accounts from the early church days. Following your readings, for each week, you will find a series of questions titled: Listen To Your Mind, Listen to Your Heart, and Listen to Your Will. In the first section, you will find questions that will ask you to think critically about and analyze the topic at hand. In the next section, listen to your heart; you will find questions that will engage your emotions and the things you feel in your heart. In the third section, listen to your will; there will be questions that will help you think practically about how to accomplish the things you've just read about.

It is my prayer that you grow closer to God than ever before through this study and that this book will help strengthen your faith in ways you never thought possible. I hope that you will learn to love others in the same way that He loves you every day and that you start to hunger for the knowledge that His word gives you.

Week 1
God's Faithfulness

Scriptures to read:

Day 1: Romans 3:23-26 (Epistles)

Day 2: Genesis 24:26-27 (The Law)

Day 3: Joshua 21:43 (History)

Day 4: Psalm 91:4 (Psalms)

Day 5: Job 13:15-16 (Poetry)

Day 6: Isaiah 49:7 (Prophecy)

Day 7: Mathew 25:21 (Gospels)

Weekly reflection:

There is no one more faithful than God in our lives. He is always there whenever we need Him. In our lives, we probably consider ourselves to be pretty loyal to those around us, such as our family and our friends.

We have been there for and have been faithful to our family members who have gone through rough times, we have been loyal to our spouses, and we have been devoted to our friends when they receive difficult news. But we have to reexamine our hearts and our minds each and every day and figure out whether or not we are faithful to the One who saved us by dying on the cross, Jesus.

God knew we would fall short of the mark each and every day, but in His mercy and grace, He still loves us, and He is faithful to us. That may surprise some people that God, who is the Creator of the world, is so devoted to us, but He loves us that much.

We might think we have done too many things wrong to be loved by God. But the fantastic news is that no matter how much we sin, God still loves us and wants the best for us.

He teaches us how to be faithful to others in His word with everything He has given us. It is up to us to want to be loyal to everyone around us each day. He provides us with the power to be faithful in our thoughts, words, and deeds.

Being faithful to Him and to others may seem complicated, but we must remember that we don't have to try to prove our faithfulness to anyone. He gives us the ability to be faithful to Him and others every day.

Listen to your mind:

In what ways do you try to prove your faithfulness to others in life?

I try to lead by example, speak to those willing to listen.

How can you change your view of God's faithfulness?

In what ways can you come to a greater understanding of how you can be more faithful with the blessings and privileges He's given you?

Listen to your heart:

Look at your own life; in what areas do you need to be more faithful to God and more faithful to those around you?

I need to read the scripture more often, seek guidance from those with knowledge and pray for guidance.

How do you feel knowing that God is always faithful to you?

Blessed as heck. How wonderful to know that He cares so much about me.

How can His faithfulness in your life increase your desire to be faithful to others?

_____

_____

_____

Listen to your will:

How can you actively pursue Him in your daily faith walk?

_____

_____

_____

In what areas can you start to be more faithful to God every day? What steps can you take to make that happen?

_____

_____

_____

Week 2
God is Dependable

Weekly reflection:

Whenever we go through hard times, we may start to think that God isn't near us or that He doesn't care about us. Sometimes it can feel as though we can't even depend on God or trust Him in any and every circumstance. But the exact opposite is true. We can rely on and trust in God for anything and everything. We should train our minds to turn to Him instead of giving into despair, especially when times are difficult.

That takes practice, and it isn't something we just learn to do overnight. We can learn to turn to God no matter what we are going through. God is and always has been there for us.

He loves us so much that He is ready for us to call on His name whether we are happy or sad. He is so good to us that He gives us blessings that are too numerous to even count. He sent Jesus to die for us on the cross and takes the punishment for our sins upon Himself.

He also gives us a free choice to depend on ourselves, on our own willpower, and on our own strength. Or we can turn to Him for dependability, power, and resolve.

At times, we may think we can make it on our own; but it is Jesus who sustains us when our physical bodies and minds wear out.

We can depend on Him every second of the day, knowing that He will never run out of strength because His strength comes from God. You can make the choice today to depend on Jesus and let Him be your strength no matter what you face.

Listen to your mind:

Have you ever thought of asking God for mental clarity and creativity in the midst of tough times?

_____

_____

_____

_____

In what ways have you asked God to help strengthen you and mentally prepare you for each new day ahead?

_____

_____

_____

_____

Listen to your heart:

In what ways have you given up your strength physically or mentally? How has God sustained you during those times?

_____

_____

_____

_____

How can you help yourself become more assertive in your dependence on God?

_____

_____

_____

_____

Listen to your will:

In what ways can you give up your dependency on yourself and be entirely dependent on God?

_____

_____

_____

_____

What lifestyle changes can you make to remind yourself to turn to God no matter what?

_____

_____

_____

_____

Week 3
God is Good

Scriptures to read:

Day 1: Romans 8:28 (The Epistles)

Day 2: Genesis 1:31 (The Law)

Day 3: Joshua 24:20 (History)

Day 4: Psalm 145:9-10 (Psalms)

Day 5: Job 8:6-7 (Poetry)

Day 6: Isaiah 63:7 (Prophecy)

Day 7: Mathew 19:16-17 (Gospels)

Weekly reflection:

God is good. He is rich in mercy, justice, grace, love, and forgiveness. When hard times come upon us, we may forget how good He is and how richly blessed we are.

We will forget that every day and every single second that we are alive is a gift from Him. He gives us air in our lungs, the ability to lay down and sleep in peace at night, and a job to go to in order to provide for our families.

He also allows us to come to Him in prayer every day, and He wants us to remember how good He is by enjoying everything He has blessed us with. He loves us and only wants the best outcome for our lives.

The best outcome is having a deep relationship with Him. You can deepen your relationship with Him by reading your Bible every day, praying before you start your day, and just stopping and thanking Him for all He has done in your life. He wants everyone to be saved through faith in Jesus.

Jesus was and is so good that He is the only perfect person ever to walk the earth. God was so good to us that He sent Jesus to die on the cross in our place. Jesus does so much good for us.

We can also do good to those around us by helping those in need, feeding the sick and homeless, and preaching the Good News both at home and abroad.

Even if you don't think you can make a difference in someone's life, the simplest thing you can do is tell them about how good God is.

Listen to your mind:

In what ways can you remind yourself how good God is in your life?

_____

_____

_____

How can you help your mind to turn to Him and give thanks to Him in every situation?

_____

_____

_____

Listen to your heart:

How can you change your heart around to see the goodness of God in your everyday life situations?

_____

_____

_____

_____

How can you make a relationship with Him an even bigger priority than it already is in your life?

_____

_____

_____

_____

Listen to your will:

What changes do you have to make in your life to make spending time with God a priority?

_____

_____

_____

_____

What are some baby steps that you can take to help others see the goodness of God in their lives?

_____

_____

_____

_____

Week 4
God Values You

> ### Scriptures to read:
>
> **Day 1:** Roman's 5:8 (The Epistles)
>
> **Day 2:** Genesis 1:27 (The Law)
>
> **Day 3:** Joshua 1:9 (History)
>
> **Day 4:** Psalm 139:14 (Psalms)
>
> **Day 5:** Job 8:21 (Poetry)
>
> **Day 6:** Isaiah 43:4 (Prophecy)
>
> **Day 7:** Mathew 6:26-27 (Gospels)

Weekly reflection:

Who do you value? Who is the most critical person in your life? Most likely, you love your friends, your family, and your spouse. What do you value? You most likely appreciate your job, car, cell phone, your house, and other possessions that you have. Did you know that God loves you above all other creatures that He made on earth?

He values you and wants what is best for you. He adores you so much that, even though you sin every day, God still loves you just the same. God values you enough that He sent Jesus to die on the cross in your place.

He values who you were before you became a Christian. He loved you even when you were doing things wrong.

He loved you and valued you when you gave your heart and your life over to Him. He still values you today even though you make mistakes.

Nothing you do could ever make Him love you or respect you any less. As long as you ask for forgiveness for the sins you committed and mean it with all your heart, God will wipe your slate clean, like nothing ever happened. He wants you to know Him and how much He loves you.

Think about whether or not you place the actual value of your relationship with Jesus at the center of your life every day. It is something that takes patience, perseverance, and willpower to place value on your walk with Christ every day.

Knowing Christ is the most important thing you can do in your life. Knowing Jesus as your Lord and Savior is the most valuable move you'll ever make.

Listen to your mind:

Think about the things and people you value in your life. What value do you place on your family, friends, and possessions?

_____

_____

_____

_____

What do you value most in your life?

_____

_____

_____

_____

Listen to your heart:

Where do you place the value of your faith walk in your life?

_____

_____

_____

_____

How can you reexamine your heart and make the necessary changes to put your walk with Christ a top priority in your life?

_____

_____

_____

_____

Listen to your will:

How can you help the people in your life see the value that you place on your walk with Jesus?

_____

_____

_____

_____

What can you do to help strengthen your walk with Christ?

_____

_____

_____

_____

Week 5
God Finds Favor with You

Scriptures to read:

Day 1: Romans 6:4 (The Epistles)

Day 2: Genesis 6:8 (The Law)

Day 3: Joshua 1:8 (History)

Day 4: Psalm 84:11 (Psalms)

Day 5: Job 2:3 (Poetry)

Day 6: Isaiah 58:11 (Prophecy)

Day 7: Mathew 5:8 (Gospels)

Weekly reflection:

When we are hard on ourselves, or we think we can't ever do things correctly, our thoughts start spiraling out of control. God doesn't want us to feel bad about ourselves.

Instead, He wants us to think positively about ourselves every day and to remember that He loves us more than we could ever possibly imagine, think, or ever fully know.

We will never fully understand how deeply He loves us, but we can rest in His assurance that no matter how hard things get or how hard we can be on ourselves, God still finds favor with us. Let that thought sink into your spirit, that the Creator of the universe finds favor with us and delights in us.

He finds favor when we tell people about Him and witness to them both at home and in our neighborhoods.

He finds favor in us when we stop what we are doing just to praise and thank Him for everything He has done for us. He also finds favor in us when we are down to our last ounce of earthly strength, and we turn to Him asking Him for help, saying, "Lord, please help me.

I can't do this on my own anymore!" He favors us so much that He will move heaven and earth to help us achieve greatness in our lives. He promises that He will never leave us or forsake us. Even when we feel unworthy to be in His presence,

He invites us to come to Him anytime, anywhere, with loving and open arms. He finds favor in us no matter how we may be feeling, and He will always see us as His beloved children. We can rest assured that His blessing over us will never go away.

Listen to your mind:

Think back to a time when you were hard on yourself. What were you struggling with? How did God help you overcome it?

_____

_____

_____

_____

How did you turn to God in the midst of your struggle? How did God show you that He favors you?

_____

_____

_____

_____

Listen to your heart:

Think back to a time when you were hard on yourself. What were you struggling with? How did God help you overcome it?

How has God spoken to you and calmed your heart by telling you that He has favor on your life?

_____

_____

_____

_____

How have you rested in that assurance that He has complete favor over your life?

_____

_____

_____

_____

Listen to your will:

In what ways has God bestowed His favor on your life?

_____

_____

_____

_____

How have you helped others in your life know that God finds favor with them despite difficult circumstances?

_____

_____

_____

_____

Week 6
God is Holy

Scriptures to read:

Day 1: Romans 12:1 (The Epistles)

Day 2: Genesis 2:3 (The Law)

Day 3: Joshua 5:15 (History)

Day 4: Psalm 103:1 (Psalms)

Day 5: Job 5:1 (Poetry)

Day 6: Isaiah 6:3 (Prophecy)

Day 7: Mathew 24:15 (Gospels)

Weekly reflection:

God is the only one on earth and in heaven that is holy. There is no one that can ever compare to Him. He is upright, blameless, and holy.

There is none beside Him, beneath Him, or around Him, that is as holy as He is besides Jesus, His one and only Son. He deserves to be praised every single second of every day. We can proclaim that He is holy and perfect.

We can proclaim His goodness in our lives by remembering everything that He has done for us. He made everything holy until the fall of man. Once that happened, He had to send His son Jesus to die on the cross in our place.

There is no one on earth that can measure up to His holiness. He is able to do many wonderful and beautiful things in our lives.

His mercies shine brightly on us every day. God is separate from us because He is up in heaven, and we are down here on earth. The word holy means to be "set apart." To "set apart" means to be different. He has absolutely no trace of evil in His character.

He doesn't tolerate sin, and that is why Jesus took it upon Himself to die on the cross in our place. Because He is holy, God always does the right thing.

We, as sinners, try with all our might to do the right thing every day, but because of sin, we fail. God sees us trying our best and loves us for trying to be better Christians and showing His examples to everyone in our lives.

He wants every one of us to try to live lives that are pleasing to Him. Even though we fail, He still loves us.

Listen to your mind:

Have you tried to prove to anyone that you're holy?

_____

_____

_____

_____

How has God reminded you that only He is righteous?

_____

_____

_____

_____

Listen to your heart:

How have you come to the realization that there is no one like God in your life?

_____

_____

_____

_____

How has He shown His holiness in your life?

_____

_____

_____

_____

Listen to your will:

In what ways can you proclaim that God is holy?

_____

_____

_____

_____

Who needs to know about God's holiness in your life?

_____

_____

_____

_____

Week 7
God is Eternal

Scriptures to read:

Day 1: Romans 1:20 (The Epistles)

Day 2: Genesis 17:7 (The Law)

Day 3: Joshua 1:7 (History)

Day 4: Psalm 102:12 (Psalms)

Day 5: Job 36:26 (Poetry)

Day 6: Isaiah 41:4 (Prophecy)

Day 7: Mathew 46:25 (Gospels)

Weekly reflection:

God is eternal. He has no beginning and no end. The number of His years is past anything we could ever find out. He is everlasting. He created time. So, whenever we get stressed out and start thinking that there aren't enough hours in the day, we can remember that God gives us 24 hours in a day and that every single second that we have is a gift.

God also has invisible qualities and divine nature, and He has eternal attributes. He wants to be our God and to have a great relationship with us every day. When we get to heaven, we will get to live with Him for all eternity.

How cool is that? Think about it for a second. Because we know Jesus as our personal Lord and Savior, we will get to be in heaven with Him for all eternity when our work on earth is done. There is no greater gift than to know Jesus and have a personal relationship with Him. He is with us and watching over us every day. There is never a time where He won't help us through anything we are going through.

Each time we go through a difficult time, we can remind ourselves that we have eternity to look forward to. No matter how bad things can get, we can turn to Jesus and remember that everything will be ok because God sent us Jesus.

The depths of His knowledge and understanding are beyond anything we will ever fully know. In eternity, there will be no more pain or sorrow. We will be so focused on bringing God glory forever. Whenever you're going through a tough season, remember that whatever you're going through is only temporary. Soon, you will be reunited with Jesus in heaven.

Listen to your mind:

In what ways can you help yourself understand how endless God's eternity is?

_____

_____

_____

_____

How can you help others understand the depths of God's knowledge and understanding?

_____

_____

_____

_____

Listen to your heart:

In what ways can you remind yourself of God's eternity when you're having a hard day?

_____

_____

_____

_____

How can you remind yourself of everything you have to look forward to in eternity?

_____

_____

_____

_____

Listen to your will:

Who can you help by reminding them that whatever they're going through is only temporary?

_____

_____

_____

_____

How does it make you feel to know that whatever you're going through is only temporary?

_____

_____

_____

_____

Week 8
God is Gracious

God's grace extends through all generations. He extends His grace to everyone and anyone who asks for it. He loves us so much that He gave us grace freely, and He extends it to us every day.

Whenever we feel unworthy to be in front of God because of the things we have done, we don't have to think like that. We don't have to constantly think of all the things we have done wrong or believe that we can't be forgiven.

That is when God reminds us that His never-ending grace covers all of our mistakes. We never have to be afraid to approach Him. That's the beauty of His grace.

We can talk to Him at any time, anywhere. We have been saved by His grace through faith, not by our works. He helped us be saved by grace because it was His free gift of love.

He knew He couldn't have us be saved by all the things we have done or the "works" we have done because then we would be in competition with one another even more than we are now. We would all be walking around having an "I did this! You didn't!" attitude.

You don't have to walk around thinking that you did more than anyone else or think that you're doing less than someone else is in your life. God is still proud of you no matter what you get accomplished on a daily basis.

Instead of being mad at yourself and thinking that you're in competition with others to do as much as they do, remember it's not a race to the finish line. It's not a race; life is a marathon. Extend grace to yourself daily, the way God extends grace to you.

Listen to your mind:

How can you remind yourself not to put yourself in competition with others?

_____

_____

_____

_____

Have you asked God to help you not put yourself in competition with others?

_____

_____

_____

_____

Listen to your heart:

How can you ask God to help you remember that His grace is extended to you every day, no matter what you may be going through?

_____

_____

_____

_____

Where can you extend grace to others in your workplace, family, and among your friends?

_____

_____

_____

_____

Listen to your will:

How can you ask God to help you to extend grace to other people in your life?

_____

_____

_____

_____

What can you do to remind yourself and others that you don't have to get everything done in one day?

_____

_____

_____

_____

Week 9
God is Just

God is just in His love, mercy, and grace for all of us. He gives us direction, love, and guidance in every area of our lives. He gives us guidance in our lives in the form of advice from family and friends whenever we need it the most.

God is just in the way He takes care of sin and the way we view sin. Because of Him, we know sinning is wrong, and He taught us how not to sin.

He knows that we will fail every day, but He still loves us and wants us to know Him by reading His word, interacting with other Christians, and praying every day.

He is just and merciful in every way. Just as He promised to be there for Abraham, He is, has been, and will always be there for us. He never fails, and He always does the right thing every time. We don't have to punish ourselves for the things we don't get done every day because He doesn't punish us for not getting everything done.

He has done everything right, and He will continue to do everything right. If we follow His example as much as we can, He will help us succeed and prosper in life. He doesn't tolerate injustice, and He will punish the unjust.

He literally can't do anything wrong. The even better news is that He won't punish us for sinning as long as we ask for forgiveness with all our hearts. He wants to have compassion for us every day and help us lead others to Him. His justice knows no boundaries.

Listen to your mind:

In what ways can you stop being unjust to others?

_____

_____

_____

_____

How can you help others not be unfair?

_____

_____

_____

_____

Listen to your heart:

In what ways can you help yourself remember how God's justice has changed your life?

_____

_____

_____

_____

Are there any areas where you need to have justice from God in your life?

_____

_____

_____

_____

Listen to your will:

Have you asked God to help deliver you from injustice?

_____

_____

_____

_____

What injustice have you been delivered from?

_____

_____

_____

_____

Week 10
God is Merciful

Weekly reflection:

God's mercies never end. He extends understanding to us throughout every second of our day. When we are protected from an accident, that's God's mercy. When we are reminded of how special we are to Him, that's God's love.

When we wake up in the morning, go to work, and return home to our loved ones every day, that means that God has a plan for us. He wants to make His mercies known to us in many different ways and for us to get to know Him on a deeply personal level. God is merciful to us by helping us be witnesses to others around us.

He has freely given us His mercy by sending His Son Jesus to the cross to die for us in our place. He loved us enough to extend that mercy to us and all who believe in Him. God forgives us and extends His mercy as forgiveness. He then wants us to be as willing to forgive others who hurt us as He is willing to forgive us.

We ask God to forgive us for our sins against Him, and He forgives us, so how can we not forgive others? He is merciful to us in every area of our lives, and He is slow to anger, and He abounds in love for us. There is a fantastic connection between God's love and His mercy.

Whenever we are suffering, we can turn to Him for healing. Whenever we are distraught and struggling to go on because of stress, He comes to us and fills us with His peace.

When we are missing the people we've lost, He brings us comfort. God's mercy can fill us every day when we seek Him with all of our hearts.

Listen to your mind:

In what ways can you chase God's mercy?

_____

_____

_____

_____

How can you help others obtain God's mercy?

_____

_____

_____

_____

Listen to your heart:

In what ways can you remind yourself of God's compassion and mercy every day?

_____

_____

_____

_____

How have you seen God's mercy affect your everyday life?

_____

_____

_____

_____

Listen to your will:

Where have you seen God's mercy in your family's life?

_____

_____

_____

_____

How can you show mercy to those who have hurt you?

_____

_____

_____

_____

Week 11
God is Omnipresent

Weekly reflection:

God is always present, and He is always with us. There is never a time or day where He isn't with us or fully invested in us. He is with us everywhere. If we go to the heavens, He is there. If we go through a storm where we just don't know how to make it through it, He is there.

If we like we are going through the depths of hell, He is there with us. If we go through losses, He is there for us. Whenever we go through struggles, He is with us. He is never far away from us and is always there whenever we call on Him, no matter what we go through.

There is no place we can hide from Him. Nor should we want to hide from Him. He doesn't want us to hide from Him in shame. He doesn't want us to feel ashamed of ourselves.

He wants us to feel proud of ourselves and at peace with ourselves. When we go to work in the morning and come home at night, He is there.

When we are in the middle of a confrontation with a friend, He is with us. When we have a falling out with a family member, He helps us through that.

When we are unsure of what to do and what steps to take next in our career and family life, He is there for us. All we have to do is ask Him which path He wants us to take, and He will lead us. He promised us that He would always be there for us.

Listen to your mind:

In what ways can you help yourself know that God is always with you no matter what situation you're in?

_____

_____

_____

_____

What can you do to help others know that God is always with them?

_____

_____

_____

_____

Listen to your heart:

How can you help others know how close God is to them?

_____

_____

_____

_____

In what ways has God proven to you that He will never leave you?

_____

_____

_____

_____

Listen to your will:

In what ways can you surrender yourself to God's plan for your life?

_____

_____

_____

_____

When you are unsure of what to do, how do you remind yourself to turn to God?

_____

_____

_____

_____

Week 12
God is Omnipotent

Weekly reflection:

God has unlimited power. He can do anything and everything. We are not able to do anything and everything all at once because God didn't give us that ability.

It's ok that He didn't give us the ability to be omnipotent. God didn't give us unlimited power because then we would be like Him, and there is no one that is even close to being like Him except His Son, Jesus.

Whatever God wants to do, He can do because He is God. God created the whole entire world in six days and rested on the seventh day. He called entire solar systems into existence, created the heavens and the earth, and separated the water from the land.

He created man in His image, even though we are all of different races and ethnicities and have unique and extraordinary abilities that no one else has.

Instead of complaining about God not giving us the abilities that someone else has, we can be thankful for the skills and gifts that He gave us. We can embrace being uniquely created by God, and we can praise Him for providing each of us with a unique calling. It is our job to figure out what our callings in life are. Because He is omnipotent and has unlimited power, wherever He wants to go, He can go.

He is everywhere. He knew what would happen in our lives before we were even born. We can call on Him at any time, day or night. He is there for us even when we may not feel His presence. He wants to reassure us that He is there for us, no matter what our needs might be.

Listen to your mind:

Have you ever wished that you could be omnipotent and all-knowing like God?

_____

_____

_____

_____

How did you change your perspective from wishing you were omnipotent to being grateful for the abilities He gave you?

_____

_____

_____

_____

Listen to your heart:

How have you learned to call on God no matter what you're going through?

_____

_____

_____

_____

How have you learned to rely on His omnipotence instead of relying on your own power?

_____

_____

_____

_____

Listen to your will:

In what ways can you help reassure others that God is there for them no matter what they're going through?

_____

_____

_____

_____

How have you told people about God and His omnipotence? What did God help you say to them?

_____

_____

_____

_____

Week 13
God is Righteous

Scriptures to read:

Day 1: Romans 3:21 (The Epistles)

Day 2: Genesis 15:6 (The Law)

Day 3: Joshua 10:8 (History)

Day 4: Psalm 11:7 (Psalms)

Day 5: Job 34:5 (Poetry)

Day 6: Isaiah 53:11 (Prophecy)

Day 7: Mathew 6:33 (Gospels)

Weekly reflection:

*J*esus and God are the only two people on earth and in heaven who can do everything right, every time. They are the only ones who are righteous.

Jesus is righteous because He sits at the right hand of His Father and because God sent Him to die on the cross in our place. Even though Jesus prayed in the garden of Gethsemane to have the burden of sin and death taken away from Him, He also said to His Father, "Not my will, but yours be done." He was in right standing with God until He was on the cross dying for all of our sins, and He cried out in a loud voice, "My God! My God! Why have you forsaken me?" That was the only time God ever turned His face away from His one and only Son to have Him take on the sins of the world for us, so we could be considered righteous in His eyes.

Because of Jesus, we have an eternal place with Him in heaven as our Savior. What an honor that is for God to make us righteous before Him and to give us a place in heaven with Him, even though we are all sinners.

Jesus forgives our sins and wants everyone on earth to have a relationship with Him. We have the opportunity to be His witnesses and to help others see that they, too, need righteousness in their lives.

No, righteousness doesn't mean shoving Jesus down people's throats. Rather, righteousness means sitting with each person right where they are, right in their walk of life, and loving them no matter what they might be going through. Jesus meets us where we're at, so how can we not do the same for others?

Listen to your mind:

In what ways have you tried to prove your righteousness to people?

_____

_____

_____

_____

In what ways have you realized that only God and Jesus are righteous?

_____

_____

_____

_____

Listen to your heart:

How has God revealed His righteousness to you?

_____

_____

_____

_____

Why did you try so hard to be righteous- for the approval of others or any other reason?

_____

_____

_____

_____

Listen to your will:

How did you help others see that righteousness doesn't mean shoving Jesus down people's throats?

_____

_____

_____

_____

In what ways has God helped you recognize His righteousness in your life?

_____

_____

_____

_____

Week 14
God is Omniscient

Weekly reflection:

God is omniscient, which means He knows everything. He knows the thoughts we think and the words we will speak before we even speak them.

He knows how many days we have in our lives, and He knows what we will do in every situation way before we do.

He knows when bad and good things will happen in our lives. He knows how to get us through each difficult circumstance even when it seems like there will be no way out of it.

He knows what we will do each and every day and how we will provide for our families. He knows when we will get stressed out, angry, lose our patience, and how we will feel at every single moment of our lives. He wants us to turn to Him for His all-knowing guidance, wisdom, and strength.

Whenever we feel as though we aren't able to go on, that is when He whispers in our ears to try again and to lean on Him for strength and perseverance. There is never a place where we can go where God won't be with us at all times.

He knows that we will fail, but He still loves us as His children. He knows when we will let our lives and thoughts get the best of us.

That is when He is at work, even when we can't see Him or feel His presence. When we least feel His presence, that is when He is working the most.

He knows exactly what we need to hear before anyone says anything, and He gives people in our lives the exact right words to say at precisely the right time.

Listen to your mind:

How has God revealed His all-knowing power to you in your life?

_____

_____

_____

_____

How did you feel being one with the all-knowing, always present God?

_____

_____

_____

Listen to your heart:

In what areas do you need to work on watching what you think, say, and do in your life?

_____

_____

_____

_____

Were you ever afraid of God because of His all-knowing power? How did He reassure you that He wants nothing but good for you in your life?

_____

_____

_____

Listen to your will:

How has knowing that God knows everything about your life calmed your spirit during hard times?

_____

_____

_____

Where has God revealed His all-knowing power to you the most?

_____

_____

_____

Week 15
God is Sovereign

Scriptures to read:

Day 1: Romans 9:18 (The Epistles)

Day 2: Genesis 15:8 (The Law)

Day 3: Joshua 7:7 (History)

Day 4: Psalm 71:5 (Psalms)

Day 5: Job 42:3 (Poetry)

Day 6: Isaiah 30:15 (Prophecy)

Day 7: Mathew 19:26 (Gospels)

Weekly reflection:

God is sovereign, which means that He is holy. He is also a supreme ruler. Some people will never listen to Him, and He hardens those people's hearts.

He has mercy on those whom He wants to have mercy on. He wants us to ask Him questions about our lives, our faith walk, and the great things He will do for us. He is not afraid to answer our questions. But He will only answer them in His perfect timing and in His perfect way.

He is not afraid to answer our questions in ways that hurt us just to get our attention or to show how glorious He really is.

When the Israelites disobeyed God, Joshua, Moses's second-in-command leader, asked God why He even saved them and brought them out of Egypt only to potentially die at the hands of another army. God answered Joshua and helped Joshua realize how sovereign and holy He was.

He wants to give all of us a sign as to how holy and sovereign He really is by helping us see how good He is in every way possible.

No one is as sovereign as He is. We can proclaim how good He is by telling everyone of His miraculous, marvelous deeds in our lives and by helping others have a personal relationship with Him. We have all hoped for, wished for, and spoken of things that are too wonderful for us to know in this life. That includes God's mercy, grace, and love. It also includes what it will truly be like to have a place in heaven with Him for all eternity.

Listen to your mind:

In what ways have you been able to show others His sovereignty in life?

_____

_____

_____

_____

How has God called you to be a witness for Him?

_____

_____

_____

_____

Listen to your heart:

Have you ever tried to prove to yourself that God is sovereign?

_____

_____

_____

_____

How did God help you understand Himself more?

_____

_____

_____

_____

Listen to your will:

In what ways has God proven His sovereignty to you?

_____

_____

_____

_____

What is the most surprising thing to you about God's sovereignty?

_____

_____

_____

_____

Week 16
God is Adonai

Scriptures to read:

Day 1: Romans 1:1-3 (The Epistles)

Day 2: Genesis 17:1 (The Law)

Day 3: Joshua 24:14 (History)

Day 4: Psalm 68:4 (Psalms)

Day 5: Job 1:12 (Poetry)

Day 6: Isaiah 61:1 (Prophecy)

Day 7: Mathew 1:23 (Gospels)

Weekly reflection:

God has many different names from everlasting Father, Prince of Peace, Immanuel, El Shaddai, Lord of Lords, King of Kings, Savior, and Adonai. Adonai means "my Lord."

He is our Lord, and we can bow down and worship Him at any time we want to. He wants us to bow down to worship Him at any time. Adonai is a Hebrew name for the Lord. God wants us to worship Him no matter what we may be going through and no matter how we feel.

It takes practice, perseverance, and love to want to worship God no matter what we are going through. He wants us to say with confidence, "Adonai, my Lord, I come before you and ask you to help me to know you more.

Please help me to bring others to know you in the same way that I do. Thank you for being the One I can come to no matter what I'm dealing with."

To worship Him with everything we have within us is not something we just learn to do overnight. No, it takes time and the ability to see the goodness of God in every situation.

There is nothing more important than to worship God in the midst of difficult times because it takes our focus off of our problems onto the One who can solve our problems.

He is Adonai, and He is Abba, our Father, and we can long to worship Him despite any hard times that will fall upon us. He is worthy of being praised at all times, and learning how to praise Him despite our circumstances will help us get to know Him more.

Listen to your mind:

Did you know there are so many different names for God?

_____

_____

_____

_____

What is your favorite name for God?

_____

_____

_____

_____

Listen to your heart:

In what ways have you worshiped God lately?

_____

_____

_____

_____

In what ways can you learn to worship Him?

_____

_____

_____

Listen to your will:

How can you train your mind, body, and soul to worship God every day?

_____

_____

_____

How do you worship God on a daily basis?

_____

_____

_____

Week 17
God is the Creator

Scriptures to read:

Day 1: Romans 1:20 (The Epistles)

Day 2: Genesis 1:4 (The Law)

Day 3: Joshua 1:8-9 (History)

Day 4: Psalm 148:2-5 (Psalms)

Day 5: Job 33:4 (Poetry)

Day 6: Isaiah 66:2 (Prophecy)

Day 7: Mathew 6:28-30 (Gospels)

Weekly reflection:

God is the creator of all things. He made each of us in His unique way, with our own special gifts. The next time you are hard on yourself for the things you think you can't do, remember that God created you in His image with many special abilities.

He created the heavens and the earth along with all the animals, insects, oceans, and fish in the ocean. If He cares for the sparrows of the field and provides for them, how much more will He provide for us as His sons and daughters? He created His Son Jesus by holy conception and had Him live blamelessly and purely on earth among the sinners of the world for 33 years until He took each one of our punishments upon Himself on the cross.

He loved us so much that He created Jesus just so He could die on the cross and give all of us a chance to be with Him in heaven for all eternity.

God is so good, loving, and kind that He created us with the ability to know the difference between sinning and not sinning.

He also created us with the desire to be around people so that we aren't alone in our lives. He wants us to have friends and families and have successful marriages, with Him being at the forefront of them.

He wants to be at the center of our lives, marriages, the way we raise kids, and the way we talk to and interact with people, whether we are at home or at work. He created us to live our lives to the fullest and to be happy. Don't think that you don't have a purpose. God created you with one. It's up to you to discover it.

Listen to your mind:

How do you feel knowing that you were created by God with unique abilities that no one else has?

_____

_____

_____

_____

Have you ever felt like you didn't have a purpose in life? What did you do when you felt like that? How can you correct yourself from thinking like that?

_____

_____

_____

_____

Listen to your heart:

How has God pointed out to you that you truly do have a gift that no one else has?

_____

_____

_____

_____

How do you feel knowing that He thought you were special enough to bring you down from heaven to earth to walk your purpose in this life?

_____

_____

_____

Listen to your will:

How can you pursue your God-given purpose in your life?

_____

_____

_____

Have you figured out your God-given purpose?

_____

_____

_____

Week 18
God is Immutable

Weekly reflection:

When God wants to say something, He can't ever be silenced. Look at how He spoke to Moses in Exodus through the burning bush. What an awe-inspiring yet overwhelming experience for Moses to hear his name be spoken by God Himself.

He told Moses that He was going to save the Israelites from slavery in Egypt by sending Moses to tell Pharaoh to let his people go. Even though Moses was afraid, He still went anyway and did exactly what God told Him to do.

God told him that He would bring plagues onto the Egyptians because of their unbelief in Him.

God was immutable in those instances, and He is still immutable today. He will be immutable forever. He talked to Abraham and Sarah, telling them they would have a son named Isaac.

He told Joseph that he would rule over his family in multiple dreams. God may not be trying to get our attention through plagues the way He did for the Israelites, but He is trying to show us how powerful He is in many different ways. He speaks to us in many different ways.

We just have to be willing to listen to what He has to say at any time because we never know when He will speak up and try to get our attention. It could be when we are alone with Him praying for a way out of a situation.

We could be with a group of people when He tells us to witness them. We could be in the middle of helping our kids with math homework when He gives us a new way to teach them. God will speak to us at any time. It is up to us as to whether or not we listen to Him.

Listen to your mind:

In what ways has God spoken to you in your life? Have you felt like He spoke to you, but you weren't sure?

_____

_____

_____

_____

How can you ask God to reveal things that you need to know in your life?

_____

_____

_____

Listen to your heart:

In what areas of your life do you want to hear from God?

_____

_____

_____

_____

Have you prayed for God to give you specific answers to your burning questions?

_____

_____

_____

_____

Listen to your will:

Have you ever had a one-on-one conversation with God yet?

_____

_____

_____

_____

Have you had God talk to you through dreams or other encounters? What were they like?

_____

_____

_____

_____

Week 19
God is Kind

God is kind to everyone. He loves each of us so much. No one is kinder than God because He sent His only Son, Jesus, to die on the cross for us.

He thought about how He could win all of us back and bring us back into a relationship with Him, and He probably thought, "what way is better than sending my Son to earth to free all my children from sin and death?"

Jesus was kind to the people who mocked him, called Him a blasphemer, ridiculed Him, hated Him, and yet He never said anything bad against them. He dined with Zacchaeus, the tax collector.

He called 12 disciples and equipped them with the ability to be witnesses to the next generation to bring the Good News to anyone who would listen to them.

He wasn't afraid to raise people from the dead or perform miracles to help people know who He was. Even when He knew His time on earth was coming to an end, He still preached the Good News of His Father and had the last supper with His disciples.

He insisted on washing their feet. Even when the people sentenced Him to die on the cross on Good Friday on Calvary, He asked His Father to forgive them because they didn't know what they were doing.

He didn't speak out against His accusers while being on trial for something He didn't even do because He knew He was fulfilling His Father's plan. We can learn how to be kind just like Jesus was by forgiving those who hurt us.

We can be kind to the people who hurt us even when we feel like giving them a piece of our minds because Jesus is the perfect example of kindness.

Listen to your mind:

In what ways have you been unkind to people in your life?

_____

_____

_____

_____

How can you ask God to help make you a kinder person and to be more like Him in everything you say and do?

_____

_____

_____

_____

Listen to your heart:

Who are the unkind people in your life?

_____

_____

_____

_____

In what ways have you been kind to unkind people just like Jesus?

_____

_____

_____

_____

Listen to your will:

Who are the people you need to be kinder to?

_____

_____

_____

_____

How can you turn to God for strength, wisdom, and dignity when someone is unkind to you? What have you learned from Jesus about being kind?

_____

_____

_____

_____

Week 20
God is Love

Weekly reflection:

God has shown His love to us and for us in many different ways. The most profound act of love was sacrificing Jesus on the cross for all of our sakes.

There is nothing God wouldn't do for all of us, and He proved it by letting Jesus come to earth and die on the cross in our place. To love us that much that He was willing to let His one and only Son die an agonizing death in our place is an indescribable act of love.

Because of Jesus and His ultimate sacrifice, we get to have eternal life with Jesus in heaven when our work here on earth is done. God has taught us that He is love, and He also teaches us how we should love one another. We can lead and live our lives by following Jesus' example.

We should be willing to drop anything we are doing in order to help someone, just like Jesus was willing to drop everything He was doing to help people who needed it.

We can be loving towards people that are unloving towards us because God gives us the ability to do so. Even though we may not feel like loving people that are hard to deal with, it doesn't mean we shouldn't try to follow Jesus' example.

He loved all of us even though we are all sinners. Even though we make mistakes every day, He still forgives us. How can we not forgive others who hurt us and love those who are difficult to love?

Listen to your mind:

In what ways has God shown His love for you?

_____

_____

_____

_____

Have you ever not wanted to show love to people? How did God change your mind?

_____

_____

_____

_____

Listen to your heart:

In what ways can you show love to everyone around you by following Jesus' example?

_____

_____

_____

_____

How can you show love to those who are unlovable in your life?

_____

_____

_____

_____

Listen to your will:

How has God helped you show love to the people that are the hardest to love in your life?

_____

_____

_____

_____

Does knowing what Jesus' sacrificed for you make loving people easier?

_____

_____

_____

_____

Week 21
God is Near

Scriptures to read:

Day 1: Romans 8:11 (The Epistles)

Day 2: Genesis 2:7 (The Law)

Day 3: Joshua 1:9 (History)

Day 4: Psalm 145:18 (Psalms)

Day 5: Job 1:8 (Poetry)

Day 6: Isaiah 55:6 (Prophecy)

Day 7: Mathew 6:33 (Gospels)

Weekly reflection:

God is near to all of us every single second of every day. There is no place we can go to be away from Him, which is actually a wonderful thing. Whenever we need peace, love, comfort, and reassurance, we can call out to Him in prayer. No matter how big or small our prayers are, He hears us.

Our prayers don't ever have to be eloquent or long-winded for Him to come near us and listen to what we are saying. He wants us to come before Him in reverent worship and to know that He is closer to us than any of our family or friends could ever be. He loves us more than anyone else ever could.

He longs to be near us every day and to fill us with His sense of belonging and purpose. But many times, we push Him away without even realizing it.

We get so busy with our everyday lives and priorities that we often put Him on the back burner of our lives instead of at the forefront of our lives.

We get so swamped by responsibilities that we forget to spend any quality time with God. He knows that life will get in the way of being near to Him, but He longs to have a special place in our lives. We have to want to make time for Him by starting each day by praying and praising Him for everything He's done.

We can praise Him throughout our day to quiet our minds, and we can come to Him at the end of our day, thanking Him for getting us through another day. God longs to be near us. We can be near Him every day of our lives.

Listen to your mind:

When was the last time you spent some quality time with God?

_____

_____

_____

_____

What can you do to make spending time with God and being near to Him a priority?

_____

_____

_____

_____

Listen to your heart:

What does your alone time with God consist of- prayers of thanks, praising Him for everything He has done for you, or just spending time reading the Bible?

_____

_____

_____

_____

If you know that you don't make enough time to be near to God, but you want to be close to Him, how can you change your daily routine?

_____

_____

_____

_____

Listen to your will:

What changes can you make in your faith walk to be nearer to God?

_____

_____

_____

_____

What makes it difficult for you to be near to God in your daily life?

_____

_____

_____

_____

Week 22
God is Preeminent

Scriptures to read:

Day 1: Romans 15:16 (The Epistles)

Day 2: Genesis 2:18 (The Law)

Day 3: Joshua 1:3 (History)

Day 4: Psalm 89:27 (Psalms)

Day 5: Job 38:4 (Poetry)

Day 6: Isaiah 40:3-5 (Prophecy)

Day 7: Mathew 19:3-9(Gospels)

Weekly reflection:

God is preeminent, which means He surpasses all other people on earth, the angels in heaven, and any other beings or creatures that walk the earth. He is able to do more than we could ever think, ask for, or even imagine in our wildest dreams.

He is able to get us through difficulties in this life that we got ourselves into and that we don't see a way out of. Just when we think all hope is lost, that is when He is working the most behind the scenes. There is nothing He wouldn't do for us as His children.

He already proved His undeniable love for us through Jesus and His sacrifice for us. God is the preeminent expert in each of our lives. He knew when we would be born, how many days of life we would have, and what troubles we would face.

He also knows how to help us out with any difficulties that we face. He also knew how much we all needed a Savior, and that's why He sent His Son Jesus to save us.

He knows us better than our families and friends ever could. There is nothing in our lives that comes as a surprise to Him. He knew what mistakes we were going to make before we made them. He knows how to help us get back on track whenever we go down the wrong path. He knows us better than we know ourselves.

That thought can scare us, but it can also bring us comfort because that means that He already knows the ending to our story. We can cling to Him, asking Him to lead us down the right path in our everyday lives. With Him, we can help lead others to know more about Him.

Listen to your mind:

In what ways has God proved His preeminence to you?

_____

_____

_____

_____

How have you come out of a dark place mentally or physically by remembering that God knows everything about you?

_____

_____

_____

Listen to your heart:

What was or is the most surprising thing you have learned about God?

_____

_____

_____

What about God scares you a bit?

_____

_____

_____

_____

Listen to your will:

What fact about God comforts you the most?

_____

_____

_____

_____

How have you helped others know that God knows us better than we know ourselves?

_____

_____

_____

_____

Week 23
God is Powerful

Weekly reflection:

God is all-powerful. He can move the mountains, split the Red Sea, make the burning bush consumed by fire, show the way in the wilderness, and make ways where there seems to be no way. He made the world and us as human beings out of nothing.

As it says in the Bible, "to dust you are and to dust, you shall return." (Genesis 3:19) There is nothing that God can't do.

There is nothing that He won't do if it is His will for things to happen. There's nothing we can ever do to stop His wonderful plan from being carried out by Him in our lives.

When we think we have control over our lives, that is when God steps into the full picture and reminds us that He is the one who is truly in control.

Think about the most difficult thing you have ever experienced so far in your life. Think back on it and remember how God moved in ways you didn't even expect.

We all have gone through life-changing difficulties in our lives, and they actually help make us who we are. A life-changing hardship can actually make us want to draw closer to God instead of chasing us away from Him.

He can turn our lives around for the better at a moment's notice and help us see the good in every situation. Even when it seems impossible to get through tough times with our earthly strength, we have a friend and a savior that walks with us, beside us, and rides every single circumstance out with us.

He walks through our lives without fear of the unknown because He already knows how everything will end. He gives us victory through Jesus.

Listen to your mind:

In what ways has God proven to you that He is all-powerful?

_____

_____

_____

_____

Where has God proven that He is all-powerful in your life?

_____

_____

_____

_____

Listen to your heart:

Where have you seen God's power in your faith walk? How has He influenced your faith walk?

_____

_____

_____

_____

What has God gotten you through when you thought there was no way out?

_____

_____

_____

_____

Listen to your will:

How can you help lead others to Christ by following His example?

_____

_____

_____

_____

How has God helped you strengthen your reliance on His never-ending power?

_____

_____

_____

Week 24
God is Transcendent

Scriptures to read:

Day 1: Romans 11:33-36 (The Epistles)

Day 2: Genesis 3:1-4 (The Law)

Day 3: Joshua 1:5 (History)

Day 4: Psalm 95:3-5 (Psalms)

Day 5: Job 26:7 (Poetry)

Day 6: Isaiah 55:8-9 (Prophecy)

Day 7: Mathew 5:18 (Gospels)

Weekly reflection:

God is transcendent, which means He surpasses all physical human expectations. We, as earthly humans, aren't as smart, timely, caring, loving, compassionate, or strong as He is. And we are surely not perfect like He is. He has strength beyond all measure, and He is compassionate to no end. He also loves us with such fierce love that it can startle us a bit.

He surpasses everything ordinary on earth and everything that is extraordinary in heaven. In fact, He is the most extraordinary person that there ever was or will be.

The only other person that comes close to Him is His one and only Son, Jesus. He made Jesus born out of a holy conception and was conceived by the Holy Spirit, then born of a virgin, and was fully God and fully human. He performed many miracles, healed the sick, raised the dead back to life, helped deaf people hear, and cleansed the skin of leapers.

He even turned water into wine at the wedding in Canna. Both God and Jesus exist apart from each other, but they are also one and the same person.

They also exist apart from the earth, as they dwell up in heaven. They both aren't subjected to the limitations or sins of this world because they are not of this world.

We exist separately from God and Jesus because we are all sinners. But God and Jesus are perfect and never sinned. God and Jesus surpass all of our earthy limits and expectations because they far outreach any places our minds or bodies can physically go.

There are no limits to God or Jesus' glory, and there are no limits s to how Jesus will help us in our lives.

Listen to your mind:

Did you ever think of God as transcendent?

_____

_____

_____

_____

In what ways have you proven to others that God and Jesus are the same person?

_____

_____

_____

_____

Listen to your heart:

How has God helped you realize that you have a rightful place in heaven with Him?

_____

_____

_____

_____

When did you realize that God was doing mind-blowing things for you in your life?

_____

_____

_____

_____

Listen to your will:

What is the most extraordinary piece of information that you've obtained about Jesus this far?

_____

_____

_____

_____

In what ways have you seen God be transcendent in your life?

_____

_____

_____

_____

Week 25
God Provides Unity

Weekly reflection:

God wants to unite all of us as believers. He wants us to worship as one race, the human race, and He wants everyone to come together to worship, praise, and know Him on a deeply personal level. He provides unity in many different ways in our lives.

He provides unity by letting us be born into loving families that will take care of us until we are old enough to take care of ourselves. He lets our families teach us about the importance of having a relationship with Him in our daily life.

They help us learn Bible passages and different prayers to help us walk in our faith walk when we are younger. Those lessons hopefully carry us into adulthood, and we have a relationship with Him forever.

He lets us go to school and make new friends to play with while we are still young, and some of those friendships extend long into our lives after we grow up.

Having Godly friends creates unity between us and others. It gives us a chance and a safe space to share our deepest thoughts and secrets with them without fearing ridicule.

The most important piece of unity that is even more important than being united with our friends and families is being united as one with Christ Himself.

Even though our parents, siblings, friends, and even our teachers can play a big part in how well we get to know Christ, it is our responsibility to want to know God on a deeply personal level.

It's also our job to work on having a personal relationship with Him. He wants us to be united with Him in thought, word, and deed.

Listen to your mind:

In what ways can you be united with God?

_____

_____

_____

_____

In what ways have you been united with God through your relationships with friends and family?

_____

_____

_____

_____

Listen to your heart:

What is your favorite part of being united with God daily?

_____

_____

_____

_____

What is the most surprising thing about unity with your friends and family?

_____

_____

_____

_____

What have they done to help your relationship with God?

_____

_____

_____

Listen to your will:

Have you been able to help others be united with God in their lives?

_____

_____

_____

_____

How have you been united with God in thought, word, and deed lately?

_____

_____

_____

_____

Week 26
God is Victorious

Weekly reflection:

God has given us victory in every area of our lives. No matter what we are doing or where we are in our lives, we can see victory because of our faith in Jesus. Everywhere we look, we have victories in our lives because of Him.

We are saved by faith, and we have eternity to look forward to in heaven, no matter how hard things can get here on earth. When Jesus rose from the dead on Easter morning, it was the most important victory in recorded history.

He saved all of us from eternal punishment and gave all of us a chance to know Him. On that day, Jesus gave us victory over sin and death. Even today, He is giving us victories.

There are victories all around us every single day. We just have to know where to look. The breath we take every day is a victory because God has given us another day to live to the fullest and to live it for Him. Our jobs give us victories to provide for our families.

We can have victories in our families just by talking with God every day. We can pray with our families before our days get busy.

At work, when we aren't sure how to get through obstacles, He gives us the clarity and peace of mind to handle specific problems.

He gives us the ability to help our children through their struggles with homework and become victorious on the other side of tests they take.

God provides victories in our marriages by helping us love our spouses with the same love that He shows us. God is victorious in everything He does because He is the only one who can't fail or make a mistake.

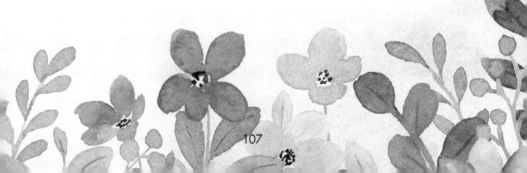

Listen to your mind:

What victories have you been given by God in your life?

_____

_____

_____

_____

Has God given you a victory when you least expected a miracle?

_____

_____

_____

_____

Listen to your heart:

What victories have you seen in your life through knowing what Jesus has done for you?

_____

_____

_____

_____

How has God helped you be victorious with your family, in your job, and in your marriage?

_____

_____

_____

_____

Listen to your will:

In what ways can you help others be victorious through Christ?

_____

_____

_____

_____

In what ways have you asked God to give you victories?

_____

_____

_____

_____

Week 27
God is Veracious

Scriptures to read:

Day 1: Romans 1:25 (The Epistles)

Day 2: Genesis 9:9-11 (The Law)

Day 3: Joshua 8:34 (History)

Day 4: Psalm 31:5 (Psalms)

Day 5: Job 1:22 (Poetry)

Day 6: Isaiah 65:16 (Prophecy)

Day 7: Mathew 6:26 (Gospels)

Weekly reflection:

God is veracious, which means He isn't afraid to speak the truth. He spoke the truth to Adam and Eve after they disobeyed Him and sinned.

He told them that they would be banished from the Garden of Eden and that He would greatly increase Eve's pains in childbirth.

He told them that He would be with them even though they made a mistake. He kept His word with Abraham when Abraham and Sarah took matters into their own hands so they would have a child. He told the truth and still let them eventually give birth to Isaac.

When Joseph was thrown in prison for a crime he didn't commit; God was still with Him. He gave Joseph the ability to interpret dreams, and Joseph then interpreted two prisoners' dreams. Later on, Joseph was able to save all of Egypt from famine because Pharoah asked him to interpret one of his dreams, and Joseph was able to.

At the time, Joseph didn't expect to see his brothers ever again, but God made him a leader over all of Egypt, and he was able to forgive his brothers for selling him into slavery. God spoke the truth to all of those people.

God speaks the truth over our lives today. He shows His love for us every day and wants us to know that He will never leave us or forsake us.

He helps us know His truth by reading the Bible and by going to church and listening to what He tells us in the stillness of our hearts. He isn't afraid to speak the truth. He wants us to speak the truth about Him and what He has done for us to anyone who will listen.

Listen to your mind:

In what ways has God spoken the truth in your life?

_____

_____

_____

In what ways has God helped you not be afraid to speak the truth?

_____

_____

_____

Listen to your heart:

Have you heard Jesus speaking the truth to you in the stillness of your heart? What was it like for you?

_____

_____

_____

What was or is your favorite piece of truth that you have ever received from God?

_____

_____

_____

_____

Listen to your will:

In what ways can you speak God's truth and tell people who He is and what He has done?

_____

_____

_____

_____

When do you think is the best time for you to start speaking God's truth over your life or in your friends or your family's life?

_____

_____

_____

Week 28
God is Wise

Scriptures to read:

Day 1: Romans 16:19 (The Epistles)

Day 2: Genesis 50:19-21 (The Law)

Day 3: Joshua 23:6 (History)

Day 4: Psalm 19:7 (Psalms)

Day 5: Job 12:12 (Poetry)

Day 6: Isaiah 25:4 (Prophecy)

Day 7: Mathew 10:17 (Gospels)

Weekly reflection:

God is wise beyond our understanding and wise beyond our ability to know. He wants us to know how wise He is. Think about it.

There is nothing that He doesn't know, and there is nothing that He won't do for us as His children. He wants us to be wise with our finances, in our marriages, and in the way we talk to our spouses and children.

He wants us to know how to approach everyone with love. He wants us to know how to approach every situation appropriately. In our lives, we probably consider ourselves pretty wise in how we handle everyday life situations.

At times, we might even think we know it all when it comes to our fiancés, our marriages, how to raise our children, and how we should behave at work.

We often think too highly of ourselves and think that we may not need any more wisdom. But we have to reexamine our hearts and our minds and ask ourselves what we really need to learn.

We can learn to be wiser in our interactions with our families, with our spouses, in our marriages, and when we are at work. We can also learn to be wiser and smarter with our finances.

We can learn to be wise with all of the gifts God has given us, including how to interact with our families in love, how to approach problems at work with professionalism, and how to approach issues that we may have with our children and our spouse.

God also helps us become wiser by knowing how to control our finances every year. We can learn to be wise in all of these situations by listening to what God is telling us to do.

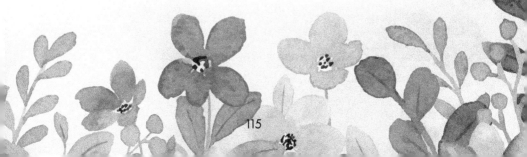

Listen to your mind:

In what ways do you consider yourself to be wise in different areas of your life?

_____

_____

_____

_____

Have you ever thought too highly of yourself and thought that you might not need any more wisdom?

_____

_____

_____

_____

Listen to your heart:

What have you done to help yourself be wiser in your finances, with your family, in your marriage, and at work?

_____

_____

_____

_____

In what ways has God helped you become wiser in all of those areas of your life?

_____

_____

_____

_____

Listen to your will:

In what ways has God allowed you to humble yourself and realize that you still have plenty to learn?

_____

_____

_____

_____

What lessons has God helped you learn throughout your life? What lessons do you want Him to help you learn in your future?

_____

_____

_____

_____

Week 29
God is Zealous

Scriptures to read:

Day 1: Romans 12:11 (The Epistles)

Day 2: Genesis 6:6 (The Law)

Day 3: Joshua 24:19 (History)

Day 4: Psalm 78:58 (Psalms)

Day 5: Job 1:5 (Poetry)

Day 6: Isaiah 42:8 (Prophecy)

Day 7: Mathew 26:52 (Gospels)

Weekly reflection:

God is zealous for each of us as His children. He is so happy when someone comes to know Him as their Lord and Savior. There is nothing more that makes Him happier than to see His children be saved.

There is nothing that He won't do to help us know Jesus. He helps us when we need it the most. When we think we can't go on, He lifts us up with strength and determination to continue the good fight.

We can also be zealous in our pursuit of Him in our everyday lives by pursuing Him with everything we have. We can pursue Him and get to know Him by reading His Word every day and by going to church every week.

We can also get to know Him by spending time with other Christians. We can also have a great zeal when witnessing other people who may not know Him.

We can be happy when we get the opportunity to witness to people and tell them about what God has done in our lives.

When God gives us the ability to witness to others, we can jump at every opportunity. When we help others know Him, He smiles and says, "well done, good and faithful servant."

We can be proud of helping others have a personal relationship with Him. There is no better privilege than to help the people in our lives know Jesus. He is zealous about knowing us, so how can we not be zealous and happy about knowing Him?

Listen to your mind:

When was the last time you were zealous about anything in your life?

_____

_____

_____

_____

How has God changed your perspective and allowed you to be zealous about leading others to Him?

_____

_____

_____

Listen to your heart:

In what ways have you shown your eagerness to witness to people who need it the most?

_____

_____

_____

_____

How have you felt when you help others know Him personally?

_____

_____

_____

_____

Listen to your will:

How can you help yourself be more eager to know God in every area of your life?

_____

_____

_____

_____

How can you help yourself enjoy witnessing even more?

_____

_____

_____

_____

Week 30
God is Unchangeable

Scriptures to read:

Day 1: Romans 11:29 (The Epistles)

Day 2: Genesis 1:1 (The Law)

Day 3: Joshua 23:14 (History)

Day 4: Psalm 33:7 (Psalms)

Day 5: Job 23:13 (Poetry)

Day 6: Isaiah 44:6 (Prophecy)

Day 7: Mathew 28:18 (Gospels)

Weekly reflection:

God is unchangeable because He is Alpha and Omega, the beginning and the end. He created the earth and everything in it.

Nothing we do will ever change His love for us, which is amazing. He tells us in His word that He doesn't change. Unlike Him, we can do a lot to change our ways in every area of our lives.

We often think we know how to handle things on our own, but the reality of it is that we need to look at the big picture of our lives.

We can reexamine our lives and know that there are areas that we need to change. We can change from talking to people with an edge in our voices to talking to people with love in our voices. Instead of complaining about our jobs, we can turn our attitude around and be thankful that God gave us a job.

Instead of complaining about everything that our spouse doesn't do, we can try focusing on the great qualities of our spouse that made us fall in love with them in the first place.

Instead of being mad at our children for not cleaning up their rooms, we can ask God to help soften our hearts toward them and meet them right where they are. Instead of automatically judging someone that we don't know, we can smile at them.

Instead of being upset that we have to do house chores, we can think of how we get to do chores and the fact that we actually have a house to clean.

Everything that we have is a blessing, and we can thank God that He gives us the ability to change our feelings about any situation around us.

Listen to your mind:

In what ways do you need to change your attitude around in your life?

_____

_____

_____

_____

Have you ever thought that you didn't need to change?

_____

_____

_____

_____

Listen to your heart:

How has God helped soften your heart towards your spouse, children, or even a stranger that you saw?

_____

_____

_____

_____

In what ways have you been able to change the way you view housework?

_____

_____

_____

_____

Listen to your will:

In what ways has God helped you know how blessed you are?

_____

_____

_____

_____

How have you been able to change the way you talk to people every day?

_____

_____

_____

Week 31
God is Spiritual

Scriptures to read:

Day 1: Romans 8:6 (The Epistles)

Day 2: Genesis 1:2 (The Law)

Day 3: Joshua 22:5 (History)

Day 4: Psalm 1:2 (Psalms)

Day 5: Job 32:8 (Poetry)

Day 6: Isaiah 26:3 (Prophecy)

Day 7: Mathew 27:42-46 (Gospels)

Weekly reflection:

God is spiritual in different ways. He is a person, the Holy Spirit, and fully human, all in one. He is the Holy Spirit because He dwells among us every day, no matter where we are or what we are doing. He is omnipresent and is always with us.

Jesus told the disciples that even though He was leaving them to go back up into heaven, there would still be a helper for them every day of their lives. That helper was the Holy Spirit. The Holy Spirit came over all the disciples at Pentecost in tongues of fire, enabling them to speak many different languages even though they didn't know the languages they were speaking from memory.

God is also spiritual in the way He wanted to save us all from ourselves by sending Jesus into our lives and in our hearts. He wants every single one of us to be saved, not by our own works but by faith alone.

Jesus was and is spiritual because He taught everyone around Him about the goodness and love of God the Father. He taught people in parables so they could listen and understand what He was telling them. It's the same way He teaches us today in His word.

God is spiritual in church and outside of the church. We can feel His presence in worship music, by listening to sermons, and by immersing ourselves in His word. God and Jesus even feel the same emotions that we feel on a daily basis.

When we are upset, they both feel our sadness. When we are mad, they want to comfort and calm us. When we don't know how to go on, they both whisper, "try again," through the Holy Spirit in our hearts.

Listen to your mind:

In what ways can you be more open-minded about the Holy Spirit?

_____

_____

_____

_____

What is your favorite Bible passage about God being spiritual?

_____

_____

_____

_____

Listen to your heart:

How has God led you on your spiritual path?

_____

_____

_____

_____

What has that journey of spirituality been like for you?

_____

_____

_____

_____

Listen to your will:

In what ways have you embraced God's spirit in your life? How can you learn to embrace His spirit every day at a moment's notice?

_____

_____

_____

_____

In what ways can you help lead others to know about Jesus, God, and the Holy Spirit?

_____

_____

_____

Week 32
God is Invisible

Weekly reflection:

God is invisible, which means He can't be seen or heard in human form. But He can be seen and heard in spiritual form.

We can hear Him talking to us when we call on Him in prayer, when we engage in worship, listen to worship music, or even when we spend quiet time out in nature reading our Bibles.

We can also feel His presence when we witness to others His great glory. People we talk to might wonder how we could worship a God that is invisible.

A lot of people will be confused as to why and how we worship someone who is unseen. But that gives us the awesome privilege of helping them understand who He really is to us.

We can explain to them that just because we don't see Him or hear Him in the physical sense, in the way we see our friends and family, doesn't mean He doesn't exist.

The only person who has actually seen God in the flesh is Jesus. Jesus has been working side-by-side with His Father since He was given His divine assignment to save all the earth from eternal punishment. Even though we haven't physically seen Jesus in our lives, we feel His presence whenever a friend comforts us with a hug, when we call on His name in prayer, in thanksgiving, or when we need strength.

We will eventually see both God and Jesus when He calls us home to heaven to be with Him. Just because God is invisible doesn't mean that He isn't working on our lives at every moment of every day.

He can be both seen and heard when we do our best to live by His example and spread His Good News both at home and around our community.

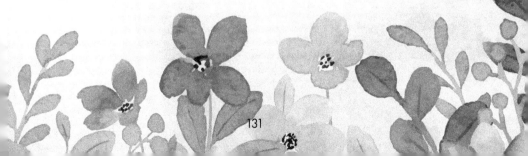

Listen to your mind:

In what ways have you felt God's presence in your life, even though He can't be seen?

_____

_____

_____

_____

How have you heard God speaking to you throughout your life?

_____

_____

_____

Listen to your heart:

In what ways have you heard Him speak to your heart?

_____

_____

_____

_____

In what ways were/are you able to witness to others about Him?

_____

_____

_____

_____

Listen to your will:

When was the most intimate time you have ever had with God so far in your life?

_____

_____

_____

_____

In what ways have you seen Him working in your life and in others' lives?

_____

_____

_____

_____

Week 33
God is Truthful

Scriptures to read:

Day 1: Romans 1:18 (The Epistles)

Day 2: Genesis 42:16 (The Law)

Day 3: Joshua 21:45 (History)

Day 4: Psalm 145:18 (Psalms)

Day 5: Job 34:12 (Poetry)

Day 6: Isaiah 43:1-5 (Prophecy)

Day 7: Mathew 6:33 (Gospels)

Weekly reflection:

God is always truthful to us. He lets us know when we have done wrong and when He is proud of us for doing and saying the right things. Whenever He wants something to be known, nothing can stop Him from making it known.

He wants everyone on earth to know that He is the way, truth, and life. No one can come to the Father except through Jesus. God speaks the truth over us every day.

We just have to know where to obtain His truth. We can obtain His truth by reading His word every day, praying, and by seeking Him out. God is the only one who can be one hundred percent truthful because He is without sin.

We are not without sin, and we can't always be truthful. We try to be truthful in the words we speak and, in the things, we do towards others, but we will fail every day because of sin.

Whenever we are tempted to tell a little white lie to someone because we think it will do no harm, that is when we often get caught up thinking about right and wrong. God gave us the ability to know the difference between right and wrong.

He also gave us the ability to tell the truth to everyone we interact with and to tell ourselves the truth. We can reexamine our hearts to keep God's truth in the forefront. We have to ask ourselves whether we are truthful to God and to those around us.

God will always be blunt with His truth. That may surprise some people, but He is always going to be straightforward with us and tell us what we should do and how we should act like His children.

Listen to your mind:

In what ways have you been truthful to God and to others in your life?

_____

_____

_____

_____

In what ways have you fallen short of speaking God's truth?

_____

_____

_____

_____

Listen to your heart:

What is your favorite piece of truth that you can tell others about God?

_____

_____

_____

_____

How has God convicted you to always tell the truth?

_____

_____

_____

_____

Listen to your will:

In what ways can you teach others to be truthful?

_____

_____

_____

_____

In what ways can you speak God's truth to everyone around you?

_____

_____

_____

_____

Week 34
God is Patient

Weekly reflection:

God is patient with us all of the time. Even though we sin every day, He still loves us and wants to know us as His children. He is even better than our parents and family members in being patient because He is the ultimate example of a patient, loving parent. He is patient in the way He talks to us and in the way, He shows us His love.

He doesn't force His love on us. Rather, He gives each of us the free will to choose Him. We have the opportunity to choose whether or not to follow Him. Even though we fail in every way, we don't have to fear His wrath and punishment because of His love, forgiveness, and grace towards us. Just like a parent shows unconditional love and patience, God shows us His unconditional love and patience.

He doesn't lose His cool with us like our parents, and family members sometimes do. When we wander far from Him, He is never far away from us.

He is always ready to call us back into His loving, open arms at a moment's notice. He is actually waiting patiently for us to return to Him.

He wants us to seek Him with all our hearts. He wants us to let people know that He is waiting for us patiently to get to know Him again.

He is always patient with us no matter what we are doing. When we don't know which path to take, He gently guides us without pressuring us.

When we are wandering, He gets us back on His path. When we aren't patient enough with ourselves, He reminds us that we don't have to do everything at once. Through Him, we can be patient with ourselves.

Listen to your mind:

In what ways have you noticed that God has been patient with you?

_____

_____

_____

_____

In what ways can you be more patient with others around you and with yourself?

_____

_____

_____

_____

Listen to your heart:

How have you helped others know that God is always willing to welcome them back with open arms when they are led astray?

_____

_____

_____

_____

How have you shown God patience when He doesn't answer your prayers in the way that you'd like them to be answered?

_____

_____

_____

_____

Listen to your will:

How can you continually trust that God has a plan for your life, even if you don't understand it?

_____

_____

_____

_____

In what ways can you remind yourself that God is constantly patient with you?

_____

_____

_____

_____

Week 35
God is Peaceful

Weekly reflection:

God is peaceful in every sense of the word. When our hearts and minds are filled with fear and dread, He gives us His peace; we need it the most.

He gives peace to us whenever we pray for it, and He delivers us from our fears and insecurities. He gives us peace when we listen to worship music and helps our hearts and minds become peaceful places to dwell in.

He doesn't want us to be worked up and in distress all the time. Rather, He wants us to live in peace every day of our lives. When we are in distress, it makes Him sad. It actually breaks His heart when we are upset, angry, and in any form of distress.

He wants us to be able to go about every day in peace and to find joy in our lives. He is the ultimate Prince of Peace and the only way we can find true peace.

He wants us to live in peace with everyone we know. He also wants us to give other people peace when they are going through hard times.

We can remember how Jesus has given us peace during our most difficult times and how He has gotten us through situations where there seemed to be no hope.

There is always a reason to be peaceful in life. We can help others be peaceful when they are struggling to find peace within themselves or within their families.

We can also help ourselves realize that we don't have to be at war with ourselves. We can remind ourselves that it is OK to call on God to give us His peace that transcends all understanding.

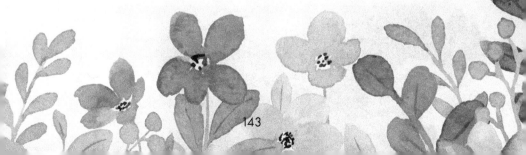

Listen to your mind:

In what ways can you bring peace to yourself and your family?

_____

_____

_____

In what ways have you been given peace in your life?

_____

_____

_____

Listen to your heart:

In what ways have you helped others find the peace from God that they desperately need?

_____

_____

_____

Where and when have you felt God giving you the peace that you need the most?

_____

_____

_____

_____

Listen to your will:

In what ways can you help others find the peace within themselves that they are searching for?

_____

_____

_____

_____

In what ways can you help yourself embrace God's peace every day?

_____

_____

_____

Week 36
God Wants to Know Us

Weekly reflection:

God is jealous because He loves us. He wants us to know Him personally and to know what He can do for us. He wants everyone to know Him and how much He loves us. Even though hearing that He can be wrathful can sometimes scare us, it should also motivate us to do the right thing in every situation.

We can be jealous of our friends, family, and their successes. We can compare ourselves to other people and their success. Comparison is the thief of joy. God doesn't wasn't us to be jealous of anything that anyone else has.

Jealousy can ruin friendships and relationships with our family members. Think back to a time when you were jealous of something one of your friends received. Instead of being happy for them, maybe you walked away in anger and refused to talk to them for a few days until you calmed down.

God wants you to remember that being jealous can only make you feel even worse. Instead, God wants us to be happy for those who have received great news in their lives. We have to ask ourselves whether we are willing to look inside ourselves and change how we feel when someone we love gets good news.

We can try not to be jealous of everyone else. God doesn't want us to show our jealousy or envy for the blessings He has given to one of our friends or family members.

He wants us to be happy for the people who have received blessings. If we are able to be happy for others, God will allow us to be happy no matter what we may be going through in our personal life.

Listen to your mind:

In what ways have you been jealous of your friends' or family members' success?

_____

_____

_____

_____

What have you been jealous or envious of in your life?

_____

_____

_____

_____

Listen to your heart:

In what ways can you remind yourself not to be jealous or envious of people?

_____

_____

_____

_____

How has God helped you not be jealous of people?

_____

_____

_____

_____

Listen to your will:

In what ways can you help yourself not to be jealous of people?

_____

_____

_____

_____

In what ways can you remind yourself that jealousy has the ability to destroy your relationships? How can you not let jealousy invade your heart?

_____

_____

_____

_____

Week 37
God Wants Us to Be Aware

Scriptures to read:

Day 1: Romans 1:18 (The Epistles)

Day 2: Genesis 19:24 (The Law)

Day 3: Joshua 9:20 (History)

Day 4: Psalm 7:11 (Psalms)

Day 5: Job 20:23 (Poetry)

Day 6: Isaiah 26:21 (Prophecy)

Day 7: Mathew 7:13-14 (Gospels)

God's wrath can scare us, or it can make us more aware of who He is. We can turn away from God if we think He will always be wrathful towards us, but we can also draw near to God because of His love. But just because He is sometimes wrathful, it doesn't mean that we should be filled with wrath whenever we are angry.

Instead of being wrathful, we can be calm when things don't go our way. When things or circumstances disappoint us, we can choose to be peaceful amongst ourselves and with the other people, we interact with at our jobs and within our friends and family circle.

When God was wrathful, He was trying to show the people something important. Whenever He is wrathful in our lives, He is trying to teach us something important.

We have to be mindful of what He might be trying to teach us. He is also trying to teach us how not to be angry with the people we interact with.

We don't have to be angry just to prove a point to someone. We can try our best to be as calm as possible whenever tough situations arise.

He wants us not to be wrathful in our thoughts, words, or actions. Being angry and wrath-filled will only destroy us both inside and out. Being angry destroys our minds and our relationships with the people we love. God wants to teach us how to not be upset.

It's up to us to choose whether or not to be angry. He is the one who wants to teach us how to act calmly in every situation.

Listen to your mind:

Is there really any reason for you to be wrathful or angry in your everyday situations?

_____

_____

_____

_____

In what ways have you been angry at people in your life?

_____

_____

_____

Listen to your heart:

Where have you shown wrath to people in your life?

_____

_____

_____

_____

How can you control yourself and not be angry at people?

_____

_____

_____

Listen to your will:

In what ways have you caught yourself being wrath-filled in your everyday life?

_____

_____

_____

In what ways has God helped you not be wrath-filled?

_____

_____

_____

Week 38
God is Right

Scriptures to read:

Day 1: Romans 3:23 (The Epistles)

Day 2: Genesis 18:25 (The Law)

Day 3: Joshua 21:45 (History)

Day 4: Psalm 103:6 (Psalms)

Day 5: Job 37:23 (Poetry)

Day 6: Isaiah 42:4 (Prophecy)

Day 7: Mathew 19:26 (Gospels)

Weekly reflection:

God is right about every decision that He has ever made. He is the one who created everyone and everything in our lives. He has never made a mistake because He is always right. He always makes the right decisions.

We may think that we are right a lot of the time in our lives, but the only one who is completely right is God Himself. He never fails. When we think we can always make the right decisions, we soon find out that we can't always be right all the time.

We find out it's God who directs our steps every day. Whatever He wants to have to happen in our lives, He can make happen. We can't make things happen under our own strength because we don't have that type of strength physically or mentally. When we pressure ourselves to do things correctly, we start doubting ourselves and our abilities.

We also think too highly of our own abilities at times. When we think we are right and people confront us about the way we think too highly of ourselves, we sometimes get offended.

We don't need to think that our opinions are always right in every situation. In fact, sometimes, God tells us not to say or do anything at all. Sometimes, it is better to keep our opinions to ourselves so we don't make people even more upset with us.

We don't have to constantly correct people in the way they talk or act either. We don't have to constantly prove that we are right. God will help us do and say the right thing in every situation.

Listen to your mind:

In what ways have you tried to prove that you're right in everything you do?

_____

_____

_____

_____

In what ways has God helped you realize that you don't always have to be right?

_____

_____

_____

_____

Listen to your heart:

In what ways has God proven that He is the only one who is constantly doing and saying the right things?

_____

_____

_____

_____

When did you realize that you have to stop trying to be right about things in your life?

_____

_____

_____

_____

Listen to your will:

In what ways can you stop being right?

_____

_____

_____

_____

How has God helped you realize that He is the only one who can constantly be right?

_____

_____

_____

_____

Week 39
God is Comforting

God comforts us in our darkest time of need. He puts His loving arms around us when we need it the most, and He will never leave us. He wipes our tears when we are crying. He comes to us and redirects our steps when we are lost and don't know which path to take. He opens our eyes to the good things in life instead of letting us constantly focus on the bad.

He doesn't let us lose sight of the fact that when we lose someone that we love, we will see them again one day when we get to heaven. He gives us the ability to think of all the great times we had with the person who died instead of focusing on how much we miss them.

Even though we are allowed to cry, He also wants us to be happy and to remember that the person is experiencing eternity and they aren't in pain anymore. He gives us the ability to bring comfort to others in their darkest times, too.

We can bring them comfort by listening to them vent, offering to cook them their favorite meal, or we can give them a hug that lasts more than 10 seconds.

By getting their mind off their loss, whether it is the loss of a person they love, the loss of a job, or the loss of a friendship, we can help them through whatever they are facing. God wants us to comfort the people who are hurting just like He comforts us.

Listen to your mind:

In what ways has God comforted you?

_____

_____

_____

_____

What was one of the best times that God comforted you?

_____

_____

_____

_____

Listen to your heart:

In what ways have you been able to comfort the people in your life that need it the most?

_____

_____

_____

_____

How did it feel to bring comfort to people?

_____

_____

_____

_____

Listen to your will:

When did you need comfort from God, and how did He provide you with it?

_____

_____

_____

_____

Look around you; where can you provide comfort to your friends and family?

_____

_____

_____

_____

Week 40
God is Able

Weekly reflection:

What God is going to do, no man can ever stop Him from doing it. When He puts His mind to something, there is nothing that will stop Him from doing it.

He is able to do everything and anything at a moment's notice. He is able to perform miracles, raise people from the dead, help people believe in Him and Jesus, and help us overcome any difficulty that we are going through.

There is nothing that He can't do. He is able to do everything that we can't do in our own lives or in our own power. God is able to help us in ways that we can only dream of.

He can make amazing things happen in our lives in ways that only He can. He will never give us the opportunity to do something without giving us the ability to do it.

He gives us the ability to do things we never thought possible in ways that we never experienced before. He is able to restore our friendships, our relationship with Him, and our relationships with our family members.

He is able to restore the church and put the church's focus on Him again. He also gives us the ability to help those who are in need.

He will also help us to know exactly what to say when someone asks us how a relationship with Him will change their lives. He is able to change our lives in ways we never expected.

We don't have to prove that we are able to do anything under our own power because God is the one who is able to help us succeed in life.

Listen to your mind:

In what ways have you tried to prove that you are able to do things that someone else can't?

_____

_____

_____

_____

In what ways has God proven that He is able to do amazing things in your life?

_____

_____

_____

_____

Listen to your heart:

In what ways can you remind yourself that you're not able to do anything in life without God's help?

_____

_____

_____

_____

What are you able to do in your life when you have God in your heart?

_____

_____

_____

_____

Listen to your will:

In what ways can you help others know that God is able to do much more than they can ask for, think, or imagine?

_____

_____

_____

_____

In what ways can you remind yourself that you can always count on God to be able to do great things?

_____

_____

_____

_____

Week 41
God is Perfect

$\mathcal{Scriptures\ to\ read:}$

Day 1: Romans 12:2 (The Epistles)

Day 2: Genesis 6:9 (The Law)

Day 3: Joshua 1:5 (History)

Day 4: Psalm 18:30 (Psalms)

Day 5: Job 1:1 (Poetry)

Day 6: Isaiah 26:3 (Prophecy)

Day 7: Mathew 5:48 (Gospels)

God is perfect in every way. He has never done anything wrong, and He never will do anything wrong. He doesn't have the pressure on Himself to succeed in any area of His life because He already has won the final victory.

That means that we don't have to put pressure on ourselves to be perfect in our lives, either. However, we constantly put pressure on ourselves to succeed and do the right things all the time. We constantly want to do everything right.

We wake up every day with the fire inside us to constantly strive to be perfect. Then we blame ourselves when we don't get everything done perfectly.

God doesn't want us to punish ourselves when we don't do everything right. He wants us to do our best at everything we do and say, but we don't ever have to strive for perfection.

We have tried to prove in more ways than one that we can be perfect in the way we raise our kids, in our marriage, in our schoolwork, within our friends and family circle, and in our jobs.

We want to be the best and greatest at everything we do, but eventually, we will fail and will burn ourselves out by striving for perfection day in and day out. The good news is that God will never run out of strength, and He will always be perfect. He doesn't want us to burn ourselves out while striving for perfection. Rather, He wants us to take the pressure off of ourselves and realize that it is ok to fail because, with each failure, we learn important lessons.

We don't have to put that unwanted pressure on ourselves anymore because God will gladly take it off of our shoulders.

Listen to your mind:

In what ways have you strived to be perfect in your life?

_____

_____

_____

_____

In what ways have you tried to prove that you are perfect at different things you do?

_____

_____

_____

Listen to your heart:

How have you realized that only God is perfect in everything He does?

_____

_____

_____

In what ways has God taught you important lessons about not having to be perfect?

_____

_____

_____

_____

Listen to your will:

In what ways can you help your friends and family realize that they don't have to be perfect because God has already won that victory?

_____

_____

_____

_____

In what ways can you remind yourself that you don't have to strive for perfection?

_____

_____

_____

_____

Week 42
God is Blessed

Scriptures to read:

Day 1: Romans 12:14 (The Epistles)

Day 2: Genesis 12:2 (The Law)

Day 3: Joshua 1:7 (History)

Day 4: Psalm 34:8 (Psalms)

Day 5: Job 42:12 (Poetry)

Day 6: Isaiah 40:31 (Prophecy)

Day 7: Mathew 5:9 (Gospels)

God is blessed at all times. He made everything and everyone on earth in His image with unique abilities and strengths. Therefore, we are blessed too because we are made by God Himself.

He blesses us with the breath in our lungs every day, a roof over our heads, jobs to provide for our families, and friends that would do anything for us at a moment's notice. He gives us food to eat and water to drink.

He also blesses us with the ability to call on Him no matter what we are going through. Think back to ways that you have been blessed by God every day.

When was the last time you noticed a blessing from God? There are blessings from God everywhere; we just have to know where to look. God is blessed because He is holy, righteous, and perfect.

We can trust in His good and perfect plan for each of our lives. We can also help other people know how blessed they can be by having a relationship with Jesus.

We can help people know what it is like to know God and to seek Him out every day. Think back to the time you started chasing after God and how much He has blessed you since then. Whenever we take refuge in Him, we will be blessed.

We sometimes want to show people how blessed we are. But we don't have to work that hard to show our blessings to others. All we have to do is proclaim how good God is to us.

Some people will be willing to listen to us and be curious as to how we became so blessed. We can share how God blesses us and how He can bless their lives.

Listen to your mind:

How are you blessed in your life?

_____

_____

_____

_____

How have you tried to prove that you're blessed?

_____

_____

_____

_____

Listen to your heart:

How has God blessed you in your life?

_____

_____

_____

_____

How can you help others realize how blessed they are because of God's grace and mercy?

_____

_____

_____

_____

Listen to your will:

In what ways can you remind yourself of all the blessings that He has given you?

_____

_____

_____

_____

What was it like for you to receive the blessing of knowing Jesus as your Savior?

_____

_____

_____

_____

Week 43
God is Beautiful

Scriptures to read:

Day 1: Romans 5:5 (The Epistles)

Day 2: Genesis 1:31 (The Law)

Day 3: Joshua 1:3-4 (History)

Day 4: Psalm 27:4 (Psalms)

Day 5: Job 12: 7-10 (Poetry)

Day 6: Isaiah 33:17 (Prophecy)

Day 7: Mathew 5:8 (Gospels)

Weekly reflection:

God is beautiful in more ways than we know. His beauty is all around us every day. His beauty is there in the crisp morning, the sunset, a warm hug from a family member or friend, the sunrise, a home-cooked meal, or in your favorite meal at a restaurant.

He is beautiful in the way He shows His love for us. His beauty is evident when a new life enters the world and even when someone gets called home to eternity. There is beauty in our kids hugging us after we have had a difficult day at work or when we get to spend one on one time with them.

God's love is beautiful because He sent Jesus to die on the cross for our sins. There is no more beautiful act of love than what Jesus did for us. The fact that God loved us enough to send Jesus to give His life for us is the most beautiful act of love ever recorded.

Even though we sin and we are dirty every day, He will never stop bestowing His beauty upon us. We sometimes want to share the beauty of our lives by bragging about our abilities or successes.

But it is God who gives us our talents and lets us experience success in our lives. We have to reexamine our hearts, minds, and our motives to prove how beautiful God really is.

He wants to show us how beautiful our lives are by helping us know Jesus. Jesus showed His beauty by preaching to the people that needed to hear His words and by helping increase people's faith. We can do the same thing. We have every opportunity to witness people and make this world an even more beautiful place.

Listen to your mind:

In what ways have you seen God's beauty?

_____

_____

_____

_____

In what ways has God helped you see His beauty?

_____

_____

_____

_____

Listen to your heart:

How have you helped others see God's beauty?

_____

_____

_____

_____

Where have you seen God's beauty?

_____

_____

_____

Listen to your will:

In what ways can you remind yourself of God's beauty?

_____

_____

_____

_____

Where have you seen the most beautiful in your life?

_____

_____

_____

_____

Week 44
God is Glorious

God's glory is evident in all of creation. We feel His glory all around us when we are out in nature, singing worship songs in church, when we enjoy fellowship with other believers in Bible studies, or when we spend one on one time with Him in prayer. We can see God's glory when we go on vacation to other parts of the world or to the United States.

The glory of God is evident wherever we go and no matter what we do. We were created to bring God glory in everything we say and do, and everyone who is called by His name can bring Him glory. It takes practice to bring God glory in every situation. No matter what we do or say, we can bring Him praise and glory.

When we get to the end of our lives, we will be lifted up into the glory of heaven for all eternity, and we will see God coming on the clouds in great honor and glory. Everyone will see His glory in different ways.

No matter the difficult times that we go through, we can remind ourselves that everything we are going through is only temporary and that our present sufferings are nothing compared to the joy and the glory that awaits us in heaven.

Heaven is where the glory of God is revealed in all its splendor. God is glorious because of His majesty, power, and love. He is glorious because of what He has done for us. He is glorious because of His Son Jesus. It might surprise people to think of someone that they can't see as glorious, but His glory is all around us every day. We just have to know where to look.

Listen to your mind:

Where have you seen God's glory in your life?

_____

_____

_____

_____

How has God's glory been revealed to you?

_____

_____

_____

_____

Listen to your heart:

How does it make you feel knowing that you can proclaim God's glory from now until you get called home?

_____

_____

_____

_____

What do you feel when God shows His glory to you?

_____

_____

_____

_____

Listen to your will:

What can you do to prove God's glory to your friends and family?

_____

_____

_____

_____

What can you do to show that He is glorious even though we can't see Him?

_____

_____

_____

_____

Week 45
God is Infinite

Scriptures to read:

Day 1: Romans 11:33 (The Epistles)

Day 2: Genesis 33:11 (The Law)

Day 3: Joshua 23:3 (History)

Day 4: Psalm 82:1 (Psalms)

Day 5: Job 1:21 (Poetry)

Day 6: Isaiah 53:5 (Prophecy)

Day 7: Mathew 10:7 (Gospels)

Weekly reflection:

God is infinite, which means He has no beginning and no end. That also means that He loves us with an infinite love that will never be stopped or taken away from us. He doesn't force His love on us because He gives us free will to decide what we want to do.

He is always with us. He is all-powerful and can't be stopped. We were not created to be infinite the way God is, but we can still show unconditional love in the same way that God loves every single one of us. Look at the ocean versus a teaspoon of water when you're cooking. The ocean represents the vastness of God and His infinite love for us.

The teaspoon of water represents our ability or, even better yet, our inability to understand the infinite love that God has for us. Compared to God's knowledge, we hardly know anything.

God's ability to understand and do things is so much vaster than our abilities. It might surprise people that we don't know nearly as much as God does about ourselves or anyone else.

We also don't know everything there is to know about God, and we never will. But it's ok because God doesn't want us to know everything. Nothing that happens to us ever surprises Him in any way. So, what comes as a surprise to us, is already known by God.

That thought can be comforting to us because we can recognize that God knows what would happen to us even when we are surprised by the turn of events. The solutions to our problems existed before we ever had them.

While we are confined by boundaries, the good news is that God isn't confined by boundaries. There is nothing God can't do.

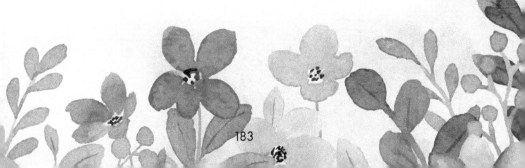

Listen to your mind:

How have you been able to recognize that God will always be infinite?

_____

_____

_____

_____

How can you help others understand more about God's infinite love towards them?

_____

_____

_____

_____

Listen to your heart:

In what ways have you been surprised by God's infinite wisdom about you?

_____

_____

_____

_____

In what ways have you been surprised by the way God knows everything about your life?

_____

_____

_____

_____

Listen to your will:

In what ways can you help others experience God's infinite wisdom?

_____

_____

_____

_____

In what ways can you help others realize how infinite God's abilities are?

_____

_____

_____

_____

Week 46
God is Praiseworthy

Weekly reflection:

God is praiseworthy. He is so deserving of praise and glory that we don't even have enough breath in our lungs to continually praise Him. We can praise Him for everything He has done in our lives and in the lives of our family and friends.

He is worthy of being praised for giving us breath in our lungs and the ability to see, hear, walk, eat and drink. He is worthy of being praised for sending Jesus into our lives to save us.

We can praise Him for the way He is always there for us and will never leave us nor forsake us. We are never sent into a situation alone, and He never gives us a difficult situation without giving us the ability and creativity to get through it.

He can get us through anything and make us stronger through any adversity that we go through. Praising Him takes our focus off of our problems and puts our focus and our hearts on the one who can actually solve all of our problems.

It takes our focus to the one who loves us more than we could ever possibly love ourselves. We can praise Him even in the midst of difficult or seemingly impossible circumstances.

No matter what we go through, we can praise Him constantly. Praising Him in the midst of difficulty helps make our relationship with Him stronger than it's ever been.

We learn to rely on Him for anything and everything, and God helps us recognize the strength that we didn't know we had within us. When He gets us through difficult situations, we often turn to Him and say, "We know that was you, Lord! Thank you!"

Listen to your mind:

In what ways have you learned to praise God even through difficult situations?

_____

_____

_____

_____

How have you praised God and turned to Him for strength?

_____

_____

_____

_____

Listen to your heart:

How do you feel when you start praising Him even when things are difficult?

_____

_____

_____

_____

How has God spoken to you, reminding you that you can praise Him no matter what you go through?

_____

_____

_____

_____

Listen to your will:

In what ways can you start praising God more and more each day?

_____

_____

_____

_____

In what ways can you remind your family and friends that God is worthy to be praised?

_____

_____

_____

_____

Week 47
God is Self Sufficient

Scriptures to read:

Day 1: Romans 12:3 (The Epistles)

Day 2: Genesis 21:33 (The Law)

Day 3: Joshua 3:10 (History)

Day 4: Psalm 90:1-2 (Psalms)

Day 5: Job 41:34 (Poetry)

Day 6: Isaiah 40:28 (Prophecy)

Day 7: Mathew 6:34 (Gospels)

Weekly reflection:

God is self-sufficient, which means He relies on Himself, and He is able to do anything and everything that He needs to and wants to do without a second thought. When we were younger, we craved independence from our parents, and we couldn't wait to grow up.

When we learned to pedal a bike by ourselves, that feeling of freedom was like no other, and we felt that we were able to do anything without help. We had the confidence of our ability to do anything we wanted to do in our hearts at that moment.

We carry some of that confidence into adulthood, where we think we can handle things on our own. We even get to the point where we think we can handle things in our lives without God. When life is going well, we think that we are able to be self-sufficient and get used to sailing through life without Him. But we can't do anything without God.

Then things get hectic and start to spiral out of control, and we feel desperate. So, we turn back to God for the help that we needed all along.

In those moments, we realize that we always need God in our lives. Our circumstances can make us realize that we need God in any and every situation. God is the only one who is self-sufficient, and He doesn't need anything from us. But He desires for us to return to Him every day to be self-sufficient through Him.

The even better news is that, even though we try to prove we are self-sufficient, God reminds us to rely on Him for that confidence.

Listen to your mind:

How does it feel knowing that God doesn't need or want anything from you except to rely on Him?

_____

_____

_____

_____

How does it feel to know that God just wants a relationship with you?

_____

_____

_____

_____

Listen to your heart:

How can you be self-sufficient while relying on God?

_____

_____

_____

_____

How have you forgotten to turn to God instead of constantly thinking you can do everything on your own?

_____

_____

_____

_____

Listen to your will:

In what ways can you change your attitude about sailing through life without God?

_____

_____

_____

_____

In what ways can you remind yourself to rely on God no matter what you're going through?

_____

_____

_____

_____

Week 48
God is Our Deliverer

Scriptures to read:

Day 1: Romans 8:6 (The Epistles)

Day 2: Genesis 15:1 (The Law)

Day 3: Joshua 1:1-3 (History)

Day 4: Psalm 18:2 (Psalms)

Day 5: Job 19:25-27 (Poetry)

Day 6: Isaiah 26:4 (Prophecy)

Day 7: Mathew 10:1 (Gospels)

Weekly reflection:

God is our deliverer. He delivered us from our sin and death and gave us new life through Jesus. He also saved Peter from drowning, Daniel from the lion's den, Jonah from the whale, and Joseph from prison and saved Mary from being degraded for her immaculate pregnancy with Jesus.

God is our deliverer from anything that is sent to harm us. He has delivered us from things we didn't even know were meant to harm us. He has helped us by delivering us from anxiety, fear, and depression.

When hard times come upon us, we don't have to just put our heads down and continue to struggle through them. Instead, we can remember who we belong and whose we are. We can ask God for help and deliverance without fear of judgment or ridicule.

We can call upon Him and allow Him to work on our lives from the inside out. Instead of struggling to figure our own way out of tough situations, we can call on Him in prayer, asking and, at times, even begging Him for deliverance from our struggles.

We are God's precious children, and He will do anything to help us to be all we can be in our lives. There is nothing He won't deliver us from.

There is no mountain He won't move, and there's no pain He won't stop, whether it's physical, emotional, or mental pain. Think about it; He delivered the Israelites from slavery in Egypt. There is nothing that He can't deliver us from. We just have to trust that He will deliver us.

Listen to your mind:

What has God delivered you from in your life?

_____

_____

_____

_____

What was the toughest situation that God has delivered you from?

_____

_____

_____

_____

Listen to your heart:

When can you help someone find deliverance from their problems?

_____

_____

_____

_____

In what ways can you help people be delivered from their own thoughts of destruction?

_____

_____

_____

_____

Listen to your will:

In what ways can you remind yourself to hold fast to your deliverer?

_____

_____

_____

_____

Have you ever thought of anyone other than God as your deliverer?

_____

_____

_____

_____

Week 49
God is Almighty

Weekly reflection:

God is almighty. He is mighty in power, love, compassion, forgiveness, and even loyalty. Think about how much He loves us and the ways He shows us His love.

It isn't just because He died on the cross for our sins, but that He can radically change our lives every day.

All we have to do is make Him a priority. We can spend one on one time with Him in prayer, and we can feel His almighty power and presence.

Every time we sin, we ask Him for forgiveness. He automatically forgives us and gives us a clean slate. We are then blameless in His sight when we ask Him for forgiveness for the things we have done.

When we sin, we normally feel that automatic sense of "oh man, I screwed up." The guilt of sin can sometimes make us feel like we can't even come to God's presence to ask for forgiveness, but God doesn't want us to be afraid of asking for forgiveness.

He has love and compassion towards us, and we are loved, chosen, and forgiven by His almighty power. His loyalty knows no bounds, and He will never walk away from us. Think of the times you prayed for a miracle, and God granted you one; that is His almighty power at work.

Think of an accident that you weren't involved with on the road; that was God's almighty protection over you. Think of the toughest time that you have gone through physically, emotionally, or mentally and how He sent a special person to be with you through it.

He is always with you during hard times. Those moments are true moments of His unending love for us. He is almighty in ways that are too numerous to count.

Listen to your mind:

In what ways can you seek God's almighty power out every day?

_____

_____

_____

_____

What was the most shocking display of God's power in your life?

_____

_____

_____

_____

Listen to your heart:

How does it feel for you when God displays His almighty love and power in different areas of your life?

_____

_____

_____

_____

How does it feel knowing that you can always come to God and ask Him for forgiveness for anything you've done wrong?

_____

_____

_____

_____

Listen to your will:

In what ways can you point out God's almighty power, love, compassion, and majesty to the people around you?

_____

_____

_____

_____

In what ways can you show the same almighty power of God and be there for others the way He is always there for you?

_____

_____

_____

_____

Week 50
God is Our Father

Weekly reflection:

God is our Father, just like we have earthly dads. We rebel against our authority figures from time to time in our lives, and we want to do things on our own without their help or guidance. We think we might be strong enough and smart enough to make it in life on our own. Look at the story of the prodigal son in the Bible.

The son wanted his inheritance, and instead of saying no, the dad willingly gave it to him. The son spent all his money and was so poor he had nothing left.

He was so poor he wanted to eat the pig's food. He felt scared and ashamed to even think about going back to his dad to ask him for forgiveness. We do the same thing to God.

At times, we walk away from Him, saying, "it's my life. I deserve the freedom to do what I want to do." God doesn't tell us that we aren't allowed to do whatever we want to do because He graciously gives us free will.

At times, we think we can't talk to our earthly dads because we make so many mistakes, and we feel like our dads will be ashamed of us. But, just like the father in the story welcoming his child back into his life with open arms, God welcomes us back into a relationship with Him any time we run back to Him. There is nothing that He won't forgive us for.

Just like in the story of the prodigal son, God welcomes us back into His presence and celebrates whenever one of His children gets saved or is reborn in a new relationship with Jesus. We, too, can celebrate that God is our good and loving Father.

Listen to your mind:

Was there ever a time when you thought you were too smart or too good for God and told Him to let you make it on your own?

_____

_____

_____

_____

Has there ever been a time when you thought you'd sinned too much or were too far gone to be in front of God and ask Him for forgiveness?

_____

_____

_____

_____

Listen to your heart:

What was it like asking your earthly father for forgiveness for some of the bad things you did?

_____

_____

_____

How did God help you realize that He would welcome you back with open arms at any time?

_____

_____

_____

_____

Listen to your will:

What was it like realizing that there is nothing that God won't forgive you for?

_____

_____

_____

_____

How can you help others know that God is their all-loving heavenly Father who wants nothing more than to accept them as they are?

_____

_____

_____

_____

Week 51
God is Our Intercessor

God is our intercessor. That word might confuse some people. The word intercessor means that He will intervene or intercede on anyone's behalf. He intervenes in our lives each and every day because He loves us so much.

He intercedes for us just when we could start making a mistake that we shouldn't be making. That is when He sends the Holy Spirit to guide us and talk us out of making that mistake. God talking us out of making a mistake could be by a small voice inside our head letting us know how the mistake could change our lives forever.

Or it could be in the voice of a parent, teacher, or friend, helping us realize that we don't have to make a bad choice that could change our lives or someone else's. Jesus also interceded for us by taking our punishment and sin as His own.

He didn't have to make that sacrifice, but He did because He knew it was the only way to save us from our sin and save us from ourselves.

He also intercedes for us in ways that we may not be aware of. These include when He saves us from getting into accidents, from ruining friendships or relationships with our family members, and when He keeps us from saying something hurtful in our moments of anger.

He also intercedes for us by helping us not be so hard on ourselves when we go through difficulties. He intercedes by helping us feel His love when we don't love ourselves.

Listen to your mind:

In what ways has God interceding for you in your life?

_____

_____

_____

_____

In what ways have you seen God intercede for others?

_____

_____

_____

_____

Listen to your heart:

How does it feel knowing that He is interceding and constantly will intercede for you?

_____

_____

_____

_____

How does it feel knowing the sacrifice that Jesus made and how He intercedes for you?

_____

_____

_____

_____

Listen to your will:

In what ways can you help others realize that God will intercede for them?

_____

_____

_____

_____

In what ways can you help God intercede for the people in your life?

_____

_____

_____

_____

Week 52
God is Our Savior

Scriptures to read:

Day 1: Romans 5:8 (The Epistles)

Day 2: Genesis 49:18 (The Law)

Day 3: Joshua 10: 6-10 (History)

Day 4: Psalm 77:19-20 (Psalms)

Day 5: Job 1:20 (Poetry)

Day 6: Isaiah 9:6-7 (Prophecy)

Day 7: Mathew 1:20-21 (Gospels)

Weekly reflection:

God is our Savior. He saved us from ourselves and our sin, and He will always save us. He has saved us in ways that are too numerous to count. When we think we can't go on, that is when He whispers in our hearts, "my child, I am carrying you. I am here for you. I will always be here for you.

You don't have to be strong and feel like you have to figure everything out by yourself. That is what I'm here for. Take my hand; I'll lead you out of the storm. You don't have to save yourself. That is my job." We don't ever have to worry about trying to save ourselves because God already has done that for us.

We don't have to worry about proving to others that we are saved because all God wants us to do is point others to Him through our thoughts, words, and our deeds.

He wants us to let the world know that Jesus is our Savior by being His example and by following His example every day. He wants us to shine His light into people's darkened world and give them the same hope that He so graciously gives to us every single day.

He saves us from thinking negatively about ourselves and from talking badly about someone else and potentially ruining their reputation. He saves us from giving up all hope and from thinking we are too far gone to be forgiven.

We can give that same glimpse of love to others who desperately need it. He saved us and continues to save us from everything that can harm us in life, and we can praise and thank Him for everything He has done and will do in our lives.

Listen to your mind:

In what ways has God proven to you that He has saved you?

_____

_____

_____

_____

In what ways have you seen God save someone else?

_____

_____

_____

_____

Listen to your heart:

How does it feel knowing that you are saved by Jesus despite everything bad that you've done?

_____

_____

_____

_____

How does it feel watching someone else get saved?

_____

_____

_____

_____

Listen to your will:

In what ways can you help others know that they aren't too far gone to be saved at any time in their lives?

_____

_____

_____

_____

In what ways has God proven to you that you aren't too far gone to be saved?

_____

_____

_____

_____

CPSIA information can be obtained
at www.ICGtesting.com
Printed in the USA
BVHW092049220722
642794BV00001B/30